the babe:
MILDRED DIDRIKSON ZAHARIAS

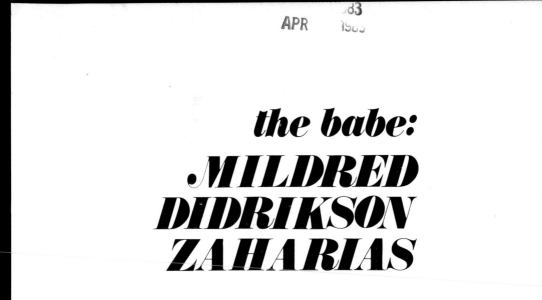

Author

Beatrice S. Smith

 Raintree Publishers
Milwaukee • Toronto • Melbourne • London

Library of Congress Number: 75-42046

2 3 4 5 6 7 8 9 0 83 82 81 80 79

Printed in the United States of America.

Library of Congress Cataloging in Publication Data

Smith, Beatrice S.
   The Babe, Mildred Didrikson Zaharias.

   SUMMARY: A biography of the woman whose
success at basketball, tennis, soccer, swimming, track, and
golf brought her recognition by many as the most
outstanding woman athlete of the century.
   1. Zaharias, Mildred Babe Didrikson, 1913-1956—
Juvenile literature. 2. Golf—Juvenile literature.
[1. Zaharias, Mildred Babe Didrikson, 1913-1956.
2. Golf—Biography. 3. Athletes] I. Title.
GV964-Z3S58   796′.092′4 [B] [92]   75-42046
ISBN 0-8172-0136-X lib. bdg.

Photographic Credits

Cover: Francis Miller, Time-Life Picture Agency
© Time Inc.

Wide World Photos, pp. 7, 16, 29, 32, 36, 42;
Underwood & Underwood, pp. 8, 10, 25, 31;
Brown Brothers, pp. 13, 22, 45; United Press
International, p. 21; Francis Miller, Time-Life
Picture Agency © Time Inc., p. 46.

1

The Didriksons named their youngest daughter Mildred Ella. A small child, she was called "Baby" until she started school. In school, her teachers called her Mildred and her friends called her Millie. They did, that is, until about fifth or sixth grade, when she began playing baseball.

"Wow! Millie hits a ball just like Babe Ruth!" one of her admirers exclaimed. And from that day on, everyone called Mildred Didrikson "Babe." She insisted — with her fists, if necessary.

Besides baseball, Babe played basketball, tennis, and golf. She also could run, jump, throw the javelin, swim, dive, bowl. "You name it," Babe once said, "I play it."

There was, in fact, no sport that Babe couldn't play well. So well that in 1950 she was named "greatest female athlete of the first half of the 20th century" by the Associated Press. One sportswriter called her "the most talented athlete, male or female, the world has ever seen." That may have been an exaggeration. But no one denied that Babe was far above average.

She looked average enough: short brownish hair, deep-set blue eyes, straight, firm mouth and chin. At 18, she was barely five feet tall and weighed only 105 pounds. Eventually she grew six more inches and put on another 25 pounds.

But it took a while.

Records show that Babe was born in Port Arthur, Texas, on June 26, 1913. (She, for some reason, claimed it was 1914.) Her father, Ole Didrikson, had been a ship's carpenter living in Oslo, Norway. On one of his sea voyages, his oil tanker docked in Port Arthur. "Poppa," as Babe called her father, liked the small port city so much that he decided to leave Norway and move there.

It was no small decision. Poppa was married and had three children to support. How would they manage?

Fortunately, Poppa was married to a very special woman — Hannah Marie Olson, daughter of a shoemaker from Bergen, Norway. As a young woman, Hannah was considered the finest woman ice skater and skier in the Bergen area. She had stiff competition, since most Norwegian children can skate and ski almost as soon as they can walk. But that didn't bother Hannah Olson.

The idea of moving to America didn't faze her, either. Always a good manager, Hannah soon saved enough money to make her husband's dream come true.

Life in Texas was pleasant. And before long, there were four more Didriksons. Now, besides Poppa, Momma, Dora, Esther Nancy, and little Ole, there were twins, Louis and Lillie, Arthur (called "Bubba"), and Babe.

When Babe was four and a half, the family moved 17 miles northwest to Beaumont, a larger town with more opportunities. In Beaumont, Poppa built a two-bedroom house on Doucette Street for $2,500. It was too small for a family of seven children and two adults, but it was all they could afford. Poppa added a big porch as a bedroom for the four younger children.

Fresh air was good for growing children, Poppa told his brood. Poppa, like his Norwegian ancestors, believed in strong, healthy bodies. To encourage body-building, he built a makeshift gymnasium in the backyard. It included a weight-lifting device made from two flatirons and an old broomstick.

The exercise equipment wasn't only for the boys in the family. No indeed! Girls as well as boys had to have strong bodies. So Babe and her sisters played with their brothers, and gave as much as they took.

One game the Didrikson kids liked was follow-the-leader. Although small, Babe was often chosen leader. And what a chase she led! Once it was into a half-built house, crawling along rafters, jumping from the roof to a sandpile below, leaping across holes that dropped to the basement.

The idea of falling didn't bother Babe. It did bother Momma some.

"Don't worry. Babe can take care of herself," Poppa said. And so it seemed.

When Babe was in second grade, she entered a marbles tournament at Magnolia Elementary School.

"It's meant for boys, Babe," her brother Louis told her.

"My teacher says anyone can enter," Babe replied.

"You're going to look silly playing against all those big boys," her sister Lillie cautioned.

"No, I'm not!" Babe declared. And she didn't. Not even in the finals, when her opponent was a sixth grade boy named Mike.

Mike and Babe had each won a game. The next game would decide the winner. Mike won the lag. He took careful aim, shot one marble out of the circle, then another; then he missed.

It was Babe's turn. She took aim. Out went the first marble, the second, third, fourth, fifth, sixth, and the seventh. That was it. Babe won the tournament.

She liked winning. The glow it gave you, the praise, the feeling of accomplishment, all of it was great. Babe particularly enjoyed the admiration of her older brothers and sisters.

The Didriksons were a close family, making up with affection what they lacked in money. Poppa earned about $200 a month refinishing furniture, not a bad salary for the times. But with seven children, his salary didn't allow for many luxuries.

They did have a crystal set radio that one of the boys made from a kit. Everyone enjoyed it, especially Babe. She used to listen in bed every Friday night to a harmonica player with the peculiar name of Castor Oil Clarence.

Babe was entranced. She had to have a harmonica.

Momma shook her head. There was no money for such a thing right now.

Babe argued, with no luck. But she was determined to have a harmonica. So the next day she found a job cutting grass. The grass was long. She had to use a sickle before the hand-pushed lawnmower would cut. It was hard work. Sweat poured down her face and stung her eyes. Her arms ached. But what did that matter? Nothing mattered except earning

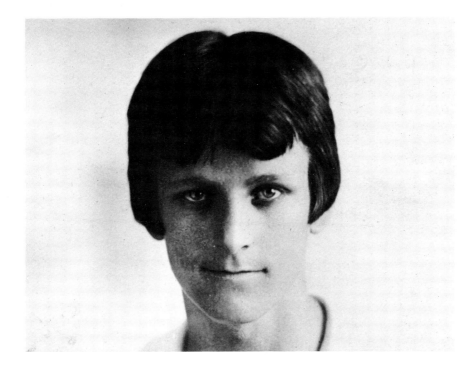

money for that harmonica.

Finally the job was finished. Babe bought a harmonica and began practicing an hour, two hours, every day.

The whole family was musical. Poppa played the violin. Momma sang. Two sisters played the piano. A brother played drums. And now Babe played the harmonica. In the evening after dinner, the musicians would gather on the front porch and play until bedtime.

Poppa often entertained his children with stories. He would tell about leaving home at the age of nine with an old sea captain who had a wooden leg and kept a chest of silver coins under his bunk. Then he would describe the trip when the ship caught fire and the crew had to swim to an island. They kept themselves alive by eating snails and monkeys.

Were the stories true? the wide-eyed children asked Poppa.

They could be, Poppa told them as he puffed on his big black pipe. He had gone around Cape Horn on sailing vessels 17 times, and had seen many strange sights.

"What does a monkey taste like?" Momma asked him one time.

"Oh . . ." Poppa eyed her. "Not as good as your meatcakes, I'll tell you that."

Momma was a good cook. The food she prepared was plain, but filling—soup, stew, thick chunks of homemade bread and jam. Everything that could become soup or stew went into a pot. And everything that could become jam went into a jar.

Poppa was the breakfast-maker. Every morning, after bringing Momma coffee in bed, he made oatmeal mush with dollops of butter on top—if there was any butter.

Budgeting the family's money was always hard. But it became even harder in the late 1920s, as the Depression set in. Poppa's work slacked off, and so did the food. Nor were there new clothes for anyone. But there were no handouts and no secondhand clothes, either. Momma accepted charity from no one, not even when Poppa wasn't working at all and she was taking in washing to make ends meet.

On the day Lillie graduated from eighth grade, Babe found out just how poor the family had become. She had been sent to the store for 25 cents worth of ground meat. On the way home she passed the playground, where a baseball game was in progress.

She stopped. And when a ball came her way, she set the package of meat on the ground and ran after the ball.

One thing led to another, and before long Babe was so engrossed in the game that she forgot the meat.

A dog came along a short time later and was gobbling the

8

last bit of the hamburger when Momma appeared.

It took only a glance to figure out what had happened.

Furious, Momma started after Babe. Unable to catch her, she slapped at her legs with the belt from her dress.

Babe protested. Holy cow! It was only 25 cents worth of meat! Besides, the poor dog was probably hungry.

Momma's eyes flashed. Sure, maybe the dog was hungry. So were people. Lots of people were hungry these days. And tonight there would be a few more. That hamburger was their dinner, a special graduation dinner. Now there would only be potatoes and gravy. *"Min Babe!"* Momma exclaimed in Norwegian. "Don't you understand?"

Babe hadn't understood. But she did now. And a short time later, the little girl found work in a fig-packing plant at 30 cents an hour. Employers were not overly concerned about child labor in the 1920s. Babe's job was to run figs through a

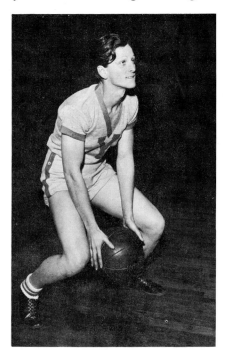

trough of acid water, peeling off the bad spots. It hurt her hands. They were often raw and sore. What did it matter? She was earning money, wasn't she?

She also was attending school, first Magnolia Grade School, then South End Junior High, then Beaumont Senior High. She was a good student. Whatever the subject, Babe wanted to do better than anyone else. Why? She couldn't explain. She liked being best, that's all. And she was. A blue silk dress with box pleats that she made in a home ec class won first prize at the Texas State Fair. She won a medal in typing class for typing 86 words a minute. She was able to figure math problems in her head more quickly than most people could on paper.

It was no different with sports. Babe had to run faster, jump farther, leap higher, play better than anyone else.

Baseball was a favorite sport of the neighborhood children. Babe loved it. She could hit any pitch her brothers or any other boys threw. And they threw some hard ones. They had to. Babe would have it no other way.

Babe also could rollerskate circles around anyone on Doucette Street, swim like a fish, dive like a seal. And after playing tennis only three days, she entered a tournament and won it.

As for basketball—while still in grade school, Babe some-times played with the senior high girls when they practiced after school. She was well coordinated and could shoot well and move quickly. Yet when she got to high school herself, they said she was too small for the basketball team.

She *was* small. Pound for pound, of course, Babe Didrikson could lick her weight in wildcats. But they didn't know that at Beaumont High School. Not yet they didn't.

2

"Too small to make the team? Is that what they told you?" Momma hugged her youngest daughter. "Never mind, *min Babe,* you'll grow."

But Babe would not be consoled. Sure, she was small. Did that mean she couldn't handle the job? It did not!

Babe decided that the boys' basketball coach, Lilburn Dimmit, knew more than the girls' coach. She told him her problem, and asked if she could sit and watch him coach the boys' team.

Impressed with her attitude, Coach Dimmit agreed. Babe was delighted. Of course, it meant that she'd have to use study halls to do it. And that meant she'd have to do all her homework at night. But what did that matter?

Nothing mattered right now except basketball. She practiced constantly — in her bare feet. There wasn't enough money for gym shoes in the Didrikson family. Running barefooted on a wooden floor caused blisters and slivers. But Babe paid no attention.

Nor did she pay attention to the smirks of classmates who thought it was pretty funny for a girl to spend all her free time in the gym. Why wasn't she a cheerleader if she liked sports so much? What was the matter with her? Did she

think she was a boy or what? Look at her! So skinny and flat-chested, wearing her brother's T-shirt, she even looked like a boy. Hot and sweaty, she smelled like one, too. And wasn't that *hair* on her legs? Didn't she know that girls were supposed to be sweet and dainty? No wonder she didn't have a boyfriend!

Babe was aware of the remarks. True, she didn't have a boyfriend. And she wasn't sweet and dainty all the time. How could a person be sweet and dainty while playing basketball, for heaven's sake? But that didn't mean she wasn't a girl. She was—and a lonely one sometimes. It couldn't be helped. Making friends took time and effort, neither of which Babe was willing to give.

She didn't worry about it. She was too busy practicing free throws. She was determined to make the team. But that wasn't all.

It was 1928, and the Olympic Games were being held in Amsterdam. Babe read about them in the newspapers. Athletes came from all over the world to compete, to see who was best, to win a gold medal.

"Next year, I'm going to be in the Olympics," she announced to her family.

Poppa smiled. She couldn't do that. The Olympics were held only once every four years.

Good. That would give her more time to practice, Babe replied, because she intended to win one of those gold medals.

Since there were no women basketball players in the Olympics, Babe decided to win her gold medal in track. She and her sister Lillie began training that summer. Lillie ran along the sidewalk to set the pace. Babe jumped the hedges beside her. One hedge happened to be a little too high. Since it messed up her workout, Babe explained her predicament to the hedge owners. Would they mind trimming the hedge?

No, of course they wouldn't mind. So that problem was solved.

The hedges also were prickly. There was nothing to be done about that. Babe merely crooked her left knee a bit so she wouldn't get scratched.

Babe kept up her basketball practice, too. After all, the Olympics were four years away. Right now, she intended to make the girls' basketball team.

Babe made the team. Not only that — she was the high scorer from the beginning, averaging 30 points per game. Her talent did not go unnoticed. "Beaumont Girl Stars in Basketball Game," the newspaper stories read. "The Babe From Beaumont Does it Again." That year, her first year out for the sport, Babe was selected to play on both the All-City and All-State girls' basketball teams.

Many people saw those newspaper accounts of Babe's spectacular basketball ability. Among them was Colonel M. J. McCombs. Colonel McCombs was an executive with the Employers Casualty Company, an insurance firm in Dallas. He also was director of the company's women's basketball team. The team had finished second in the national Amateur Athletic Union tournament the year before.

Colonel McCombs first watched Babe play in February of 1930. Beaumont High School was playing Houston Heights High that day. The Houston team was made up of tall, husky girls. So was the Beaumont team—except for one. At 16, Babe was still small. But she could run. How she could run! She could also pass and pivot and shoot. Babe scored 26 points during that game with Houston Heights.

After the game, Colonel McCombs introduced himself and asked Babe if she would like to play on a big-time basketball team.

Would she? Do birds fly? Where?

In Dallas, Colonel McCombs told her. The team, called the Golden Cyclones, was getting ready for the national AAU tournament in March. He was sure that Babe could help them win it.

"Dallas? So far?" Momma shook her head. Babe was only 16, too young to make a trip like that by herself. Only when Poppa said he'd go with Babe and see that she was all right did Momma give her permission.

School officials were easier to convince. Babe was a good student. She could make up the work easily. So two days later off they went, Babe and Poppa.

It was an overnight trip. They took the train. They had no car. Poppa took the lower berth, Babe the upper. She was too excited to sleep much. All kinds of thoughts ran through her head. How would it be, competing with big-time athletes? Would they think she was too young? Too inexperienced? Too small? Would they laugh? Make fun of her? No! The Cyclones wouldn't make fun of her. Nor would anyone else. Not now. Not ever. Babe made up her mind to that just before she fell asleep.

She had a few misgivings when she saw the size of the

girls on the team. One was six feet tall if she was an inch. And they were all good basketball players. Very, very good. But, heck, so was she. And she wasn't bashful about it.

That very night, the Cyclones were scheduled to meet the Sun Oil Company team. A reporter asked Babe if the Cyclones were looking forward to the game. "You bet," Babe told him. "They're the defending champs and we aim to knock 'em off."

But the Cyclones hadn't been able to do it before, the reporter reminded Babe.

"That's 'cuz they didn't have me," Babe replied, grinning.

The reporters chuckled indulgently. She was good copy, this little mite.

She also was as good as her word. Babe was the high scorer in the game, making five points more than the whole Sun Oilers team put together. And she did it with a casual confidence that made it look as if she had planned it all along.

The crowd was amazed. Who was this little bundle of dynamite?

A high school girl? No kidding!

What was her name?

Babe Didrikson. And she was only 16 years old. Could you beat that?

Backed up by a five-piece pep band, four cheerleaders, and a dozen metal wash buckets, the crowd went wild. "Yes, sir, that's our Baby. No, sir, don't mean maybe! Yes, sir, that's our Babe no--ooow!" They sang the old song over and over.

Babe loved it. The long hours of training, the sore feet, aching muscles, the tears, jeers, all were forgotten. So this was what the Big Time was like, was it? Well, Big Time, get set. Here comes the Babe!

Babe was chosen for the women's All-American team that year. And Colonel McCombs asked her to return to Dallas when she finished school and go to work for Employers Casualty Company. Did she know how to use a slide rule? he asked her.

No, Babe said. But she could learn in a hurry. By the way, how much money would she be making?

"Seventy-five dollars a month," the Colonel told her.

Seventy-five dollars a month. She could live on $30, send $30 home, save the rest. Babe didn't need a slide rule to figure that out. Money was important to her. What's more, Babe still wanted that gold medal in track. She decided that Colonel McCombs might help her get to the 1932 Olympics.

He did. After hearing of Babe's ambition, he talked Employers Casualty into sponsoring a women's track and field team. In her first meet, Babe competed in four events and won them all. Later, in the women's state championship meet, she entered ten events and won all but two.

That year, in Illinois, the women's national AAU champion-ships and the Olympic tryouts were being combined. The women who won in the national would go on to the Olympics.

Would many of the Employers Casualty girls be going to

Illinois? Babe asked Colonel McCombs.

The Colonel shook his head. "Just you, Babe." Not only that. He believed that she could win whatever events she decided to enter. What did she think?

Need he ask? Babe *always* felt she could win. In fact, she could hardly wait to show everyone in Illinois just how good she was.

Finally the day came. Of the ten individual events, Babe was entered in eight. What did it matter that she had hardly ever competed in a couple of them? She had done well in practice with the shot put, the discus, whatever. Why couldn't she do well in competition?

She could, and did.

It was a hectic afternoon for Babe. First there was a heat in the 80-meter hurdles, then the high jump. Next it was the broad jump. Then she was called to throw the baseball, the javelin, the discus; to put the eight-pound shot.

Of the eight events she entered, Babe placed in seven, won five outright, tied for first in a sixth, broke three world records, and scored a total of 30 points — 8 points more than the 22 members of the Illinois Women's Athletic Club, who placed second.

The crowd rose to its feet as the "team" from Dallas, Texas, ran out to the platform to accept her trophies.

Babe was ready for the Olympics.

3

The Olympics. There were 2,500 athletes, representing 40 nations, competing in some 50 events that summer in Los Angeles.

For Babe, the first event was the javelin throw. It began late in the afternoon. Shadows were coming up over the stadium, and the wind was cool.

Each contestant got three turns. When Babe's first turn came, she stood at the line, grasping the javelin, hearing nothing, feeling nothing. Every brain cell was concentrated on a spot well beyond a little German flag showing the previous record of a German girl. Then Babe threw. But as she let go, her hand slipped. Instead of arching in the proper manner, the spear went zinging straight as an arrow. And it kept on zinging for 143 feet 4 inches — a new world record.

The spectators could hardly believe their eyes. No woman had ever hurled a javelin that far. Fantastic!

Though in practice Babe had thrown the javelin 150 feet, she was thankful it went as far as it did. For her next two throws weren't very good. She had torn a cartilage in her right shoulder when her hand slipped. The second two throws didn't matter, however. The first was enough to give her the gold medal for first place.

Three days later, the contestants lined up for the hurdles race. Babe was among them. Ready. Set. Whoops! Babe was so anxious that she jumped the gun.

The women were recalled.

They lined up again.

Babe wet her lips, tense, nervous. If she jumped the gun a second time, she would be disqualified. The gun went off, but Babe held back. She was the last to leave the starting line.

She soon caught up, however, leaping easily over the wooden hurdles. They were a lot narrower than hedges— and a good deal less prickly.

The competition was stiff. The race was close. But when it ended, the girl from Texas had another first place, another world record, and another gold medal.

Next came the high jump. Babe and a fine athlete named Jean Shiley were tied for first place after clearing a five-foot-five-inch crossbar. The bar was raised three-quarters of an inch for the jump-off try. Jean just missed getting over the bar.

Babe took her turn, soaring over like a bird. But her left foot struck the standard a glancing blow, and when she hit the ground, the bar came down, too.

The bar was dropped half an inch. Jean made her jump this time. So did Babe.

Suddenly there was a commotion in the judges' stand. Rules of the 1932 high jump said that a high jumper's feet had to go over the bar first. Miss Didrikson's head had gone over first, the judges announced.

What? Babe protested. She had been jumping the same way each time!

"If so, we didn't see it, Miss Didrikson. We did see it this

time," the judges declared. "Your last jump was illegal."

Not everyone agreed with the judges. Up in the press box, Grantland Rice and several other respected sportswriters said they thought Babe had been given a raw deal. So did Babe. And she said so in no uncertain terms. She was not a good loser.

Even with two gold medals instead of the three she thought she deserved, Babe was the biggest star of the Games. Reporters from all over the world crowded around her, taking pictures, asking questions.

"How long have you been training for this?" one reporter asked.

"All my life," Babe replied.

"Why?" the reporter wanted to know. Why the ceaseless grind? What kept a top athlete going?

Babe shrugged. She wasn't sure how it was with other

athletes. She knew what kept her going. The kick of being one of the best, of competing with the best; the fun of the sport itself; the thrill, the excitement. It sure beat working in a fig factory.

Did she do anything besides track?

Sure. She swam, dived, played baseball, basketball, and a darn good harmonica.

"Is there anything at all you don't play?" a reporter from the *New York Daily News* asked her.

Babe grinned. "Yeah," she said. "Dolls."

Did she have a steady boyfriend?

No, she didn't. She had been too busy being a steady athlete.

Was she interested in getting married someday?

Sure, if the right guy came along.

What kind of guy would Mr. Right have to be?

"Not a sissy," Babe replied.

There was no subject she wouldn't discuss. Nor did she try to fool anyone. She was always herself. And if that self seemed a little too cocky, a little too blunt, well, so be it.

At 18, Babe was a celebrity and well aware of the fact.

After the Olympics, Babe was invited to attend celebrity dinners, Hollywood parties. She was asked to speak, pose for pictures, ride in parades. And that was just in California.

When she got back to Dallas, 3,000 people, including the mayor, were at the airport. People stood on the curbs, waving small flags. Children shouted. Bands played. Horns honked. Confetti flew.

The following day, one of the Dallas newspapers said of Babe's welcome: "It was not unlike the reception Col. Lindbergh received when he came here after his epochal flight across the Atlantic."

After that, it was home for a while, then back to Dallas and the Employers Casualty Company — but not at $75 a month. The old salary didn't look as big as it once had. She'd had a job offer from the Illinois Women's Athletic Club that would pay $300 a month. But Babe liked Texas. Could she make $300 here?

She could. Employers Casualty matched the offer.

Three hundred dollars a month was a tidy sum for a single person in the Depression days of the 1930s. Babe enjoyed it. What she enjoyed most was buying gifts for Momma and Poppa. They had been poor so long. It was fun to see their eyes light up. Clothing. Furniture. Appliances. Nothing was too good. Momma had been hit by a car on the way to church that spring. Babe was too far away to do much except send home gifts. This she did every payday.

Meanwhile, in Dallas, Babe was being pressured from all sides. Would she come to a grand opening of a furniture store? Would she have her picture taken in a sporting goods shop? Would she make a speech at the Woman's Club?

Often she was offered cash, as well as gifts. Never having had many luxuries, Babe was sometimes tempted. But she had started another basketball season with the Golden Cyclones. She also intended to compete in track meets the following spring. Then, too, she was looking forward to competing in the 1936 Olympics. And these competitions were open to amateurs only. If she wanted to compete, she could not become a professional.

The difference between the two seemed simple enough. An amateur was a person who competed in a sport only for the sport's sake. A professional competed with the hope of making money.

Babe knew the rules and tried to abide by them. Then, in early December, 1932, her name and picture appeared in a newspaper ad. The ad said that the 1933 Dodge was the car the famous Olympic champion Babe Didrikson preferred.

Babe's name appeared without her permission. Nor had she been paid for the use of her picture. Still, the southern branch of the AAU declared her a professional.

The ruling was a blow. What would she do? What could she do? Nothing. So what now? Sulk? No, not Babe. They said she was a pro. All right. She would be a pro. And what did pros do? They made money. Okay. She would make money.

Babe contacted the Chrysler Motor Company. Because her picture had appeared in their ad, she was a pro now. Could they use her? They could indeed. There was an auto show in Detroit. Would she be willing to go?

And do what? Babe wanted to know.

Smile. Talk to people. Sign autographs. Anything she could think of to attract attention and draw a crowd over to the Chrysler booth.

For how much money?

For a new car or its cash equivalent, plus expenses.

Fine, Babe said. She'd do it. But she didn't want to go to Detroit alone.

No problem. Chrysler would be glad to pay for a companion.

That evening Babe called home. Her oldest sister, Esther Nancy, was free. She would go.

Babe did well at the auto show. She not only smiled and signed autographs, she also told jokes and played her harmonica. Though some athletes considered it undignified to hustle commercial products, Babe did not. She'd worked a lot more for a lot less.

Chrysler was so pleased that after the show they contacted an agent to arrange other bookings for Babe.

Her first contract called for a week on the stage at the Palace Theater in Chicago. She would appear with a comedian, a musical group, and a Hollywood star named Fifi D'Orsay.

Babe was given top billing and the star dressing room. She was an entertainer now, earning $2,000 a week. Her act lasted 18 minutes. After exchanging jokes with the comedian, Babe sang a few songs, then put on gym shoes and demonstrated the sports activities that had made her famous. The act ended with a couple of numbers on the harmonica.

A natural performer, Babe was an instant hit.

There was just one problem. There were four shows a day. Babe was spending all her time either on stage or in the hotel preparing to go on. What kind of life was that? No life at all, as far as Babe was concerned. And after one week of being a stage star, she quit.

What now?

"I think I'd like to play golf," she told Nancy.

Golf? Why golf? Nancy asked.

She liked the game. She'd played a little in California. Her friends there had encouraged her. It was a challenge.

Nancy understood. She was talking about tournament golf, wasn't she?

"Yep," Babe said. She intended to compete with the best. "And," she added, only half joking, "I'm gonna whup 'em all."

4

Once Babe had made up her mind to become a tournament golfer, nothing could stop her. Or so it seemed.

Babe headed for Los Angeles. She took Momma and Poppa with her. They were getting old, and Babe thought they would enjoy California. Besides, she hated the thought of living alone for the next three years.

Three years? Was that how long it would take her to become a golf champion?

Yes. She told a Los Angeles reporter: "I have enough money to last me three years, and I intend to win the women's amateur golf championship before those three years and my bankroll are gone."

Babe meant it. However, her "bankroll" amounted to less than $2,000. It had disappeared by the end of the summer, and the Didriksons headed back to Texas. Momma and Poppa went to Beaumont, Babe to Dallas and her old job at Employers Casualty.

By living as cheaply as possible, Babe figured she could soon save enough to try California again. That plan didn't work, either.

A month after returning from California, Babe received a long distance phone call. Poppa was sick. Dr. Tatum, their family doctor, said he needed an operation. And they had no money for an operation. What were they going to do?

"Don't worry. I'll arrange everything," Babe told her family. How, she wasn't sure. She had no money, either.

Could her brothers and sisters help? No, these were hard times. They had money problems of their own. Could she borrow from Employers Casualty? No. She owed them too many favors as it was. What about the rich people she had met in California? Go crawling to them? Never!

What then? If she was going to take proper care of Momma and Poppa in the years to come, plus provide for herself, she had to earn more than the $300 a month she was earning now. But how? Go back on the stage? No. She had to keep in shape if she was going to be a tournament golfer. And she was. No doubt about that!

There was only one way she could see. Exhibition work. And after contacting several promoters, Babe was on the exhibition circuit.

She played basketball on a team made up of another woman and three young men, billed as the Babe Didrikson All-Americans. She pitched with a men's baseball team called the House of David. Once she was asked to race against a horse. That was a little too much, even for Babe.

But she was willing to do almost anything. After all, she was being paid $1,000 a month, plus expenses, wasn't she? She was indeed. And by the end of the summer, she had saved $3,700.

It didn't last long. Babe was good at math. But the world of finance, she discovered, takes more than that. In an attempt to increase her savings, she made an unwise investment and lost everything. What's more, this was 1934. The Olympics were long over, and her name was beginning to fade from the public view. Requests for appearances were getting fewer and fewer.

What could she do? Her real interest still was golf. But golf clubs were expensive. So were golf courses. Wasn't that one of the reasons she was trying to earn a lot of money in the first place? Besides, she had her family to think about. They had come to depend on her.

Not knowing where to turn, Babe went back once again to her old friends at Employers Casualty in Dallas. And once again they came through, offering her not only her old job, but membership in the Dallas Country Club and lessons with golf pro George Aulbach. For the next six weeks, Babe spent every spare moment taking lessons from Aulbach.

In November, she decided to test her progress by entering the Fort Worth Women's Invitational tournament. It was her first.

"How do you think you'll do?" a reporter asked her.

Babe did some quick figuring in her head. Eighteen holes. Four strokes a hole would be 72, plus say four or five extra for the tough holes. "I think I'll probably shoot a 77," she said.

The reporter laughed. No one could predict an exact score. He thought Babe was kidding. She was, in a way. But with a little luck, she was quite sure she could do it. And she did. Her score in the qualifying round was exactly 77.

She was eliminated in an early round of that tournament, but it was a beginning. As soon as it was over, she began to get ready for the next. Weekends she practiced between 12 and 16 hours a day. During the work week, she practiced from 5:30 A.M. until 8:30 A.M., then went to work, practiced again during her lunch hour, went back to work until 3:30, then went to the country club for an hour's instruction with Aulbach. After that she drilled and drilled and drilled, hitting balls until her hands bled. What did a little blood matter? She'd had bloody hands before. She simply taped the bloody spots and practiced some more. When she couldn't see the ball any longer, she went home, ate, and climbed into bed with the golf rule book.

The Texas State Women's Championship was held in Houston in late April. Babe qualified with a score of 84 and went into the tournament with 32 other contestants.

She beat her first and second opponents without any trouble. Next came the quarterfinals. Babe won the match, but not easily. The semifinals were even tougher. After the 17th hole, the match was tied. At the final hole, Babe and her opponent both hit the green with their third shots. Both balls were some 20 feet from the cup.

Babe's opponent took her putt. A beauty! The ball stopped just at the edge of the cup. The gallery clapped in appreciation.

Then it was Babe's turn. She eyed the distance carefully, then made her putt. It was an uphill roll. The ball rolled right into the cup.

The next day, in the final match, Babe beat Peggy Chandler, three-time state champion.

"Babe Does it Again — in Golf," the headlines read that evening. An Associated Press reporter wrote: "Babe Didrikson is still America's wonder girl athlete, and probably the most promising woman golfer in the United States."

Then, on May 14, the roof caved in.

The United States Golf Association ruled Babe out of amateur women's golf on the grounds that she was a professional. They'd had complaints, they said, about her participation in professional athletics. She didn't belong in amateur golf.

Babe was outraged. How could she be a pro golfer? Holy cow! She had only been in two golf tournaments. She protested vigorously. No dice. The USGA was firm. Babe Didrikson was a professional in golf now, too.

A pro golfer, was she? Okay.

The next day, Babe signed a contract with a sporting goods outfit that booked her for a series of exhibition golf matches with Gene Sarazen, a top professional male golfer. Babe would get $2,500 a year, plus $500 for each match.

It wasn't serious golf. Not for Babe. She was being paid

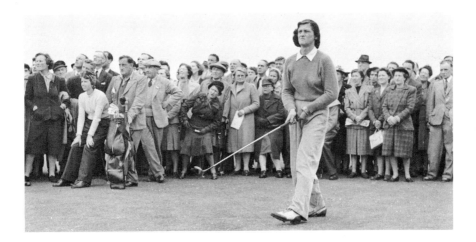

to be an entertainer. So, for the most part, she entertained with an assortment of trick shots accompanied by wise-cracks delivered in an exaggerated Texas drawl. It was a good deal like performing on the stage at the Palace, she discovered, only the hours were better and so was the air.

Soon she had enough money to go to California again and concentrate on the finer points of golf. If she didn't keep in top form, there would be no offers for exhibitions. If there were no exhibitions, there would be no money. And if there was no money, she and her family didn't eat. It was as simple as that.

Babe took Momma and Poppa with her this time, too, along with her sister Lillie and brother Bubba. The arrangement worked so well that Babe and Momma and Lillie were still in California three years later. (Poppa and Bubba went back to Beaumont to look after their home.)

In January of 1938, Babe entered the Los Angeles Open. She was 24 years old, no longer a pint-sized girl in shorts and her brother's T-shirt, but a self-assured young woman with expensive clothes and an infectious grin.

The Los Angeles Open was one of the regular pro golf tournaments on the men's circuit. However, anyone could enter. So Babe entered. What she intended to do was prove that she was one of the best golfers — male or female — in the country.

It didn't work out that way. She was teamed with two part time golfers. One was a professor named Pardee Erdman. The other was a professional wrestler named George Zaharias.

George was husky and handsome with dark curly hair, brown eyes, and a warm smile. Their attraction for one another was instant and mutual. It was not expressed in sweet words, however. Quite the contrary.

"Watch out you don't strangle me, you big lummox," Babe said to George as they struck a wrestling pose for a photographer. Suddenly golf took second place in Babe's life. She had a new interest.

George's parents were Greek. He was born Theodore Vetoyanis. When he began wrestling professionally, his promoters changed his name to Zaharias. It was easier to pronounce. His home was in Colorado, where he had once worked in a steel mill with his father. They were poor. George had always worked hard. While still a teenager, he had gone to live with relatives in Oklahoma City, and had shined shoes while learning the cleaning business.

But that was a long time ago. George was 29 years old now, and doing well. He'd built a new home for his parents, sent his younger brothers to school, helped his sisters, and still had plenty of money left over for himself. Not that he was bragging, George told Babe. He just wanted her to know. Did she understand?

Yes, she understood. Money was important to her too.

He knew she was a great athlete, but did she like to *watch* sports events? George asked suddenly.

Yes, Babe said, she did.

"Fine," George replied. "Would you like to watch me wrestle sometime? I play the bad guy." He chuckled. "The bloodier I get, the better the fans like it."

"No," Babe said quickly. "I don't want to watch you wrestle."

"Why not?" George looked a little offended.

"Because I couldn't stand to watch anyone hurting you, that's why," Babe replied, as frank about her feelings as she was about everything else.

Soon Babe and George were a steady twosome. "Romance" was the pet name they called each other.

"Hello," George would say when he phoned. "This is Romance." Or Babe might stop by his apartment. "Stopped in, but you weren't here. Romance," she would scribble on a note.

The one trouble they had was finding time to be together. With their respective bookings, they were never in the same place at the same time. Finally, after many delays, Babe and George were married in St. Louis on December 23, 1938, by a justice of the peace named Jannopoula, a friend of George's.

Only a few friends were present. It didn't matter. Babe had become Mrs. George Zaharias. She was so proud that instead of entering exhibitions under her own well-known name, she now simply wrote, "Mrs. Zaharias."

Their marriage wasn't perfect. Babe was sharp-tongued, often blurting out what might better have been left unsaid— at least as far as George was concerned. The "bad guy" of the wrestling ring was thin-skinned, Babe discovered. He was also gentle and affectionate. He even served her coffee in bed, just the way Poppa did for Momma. Babe loved him very much.

5

After a honeymoon in Hawaii and Australia, Babe and George returned to California. What would Babe do now? Stay home, bake, sew, grow roses, have children? It sounded fine to both Babe and George, especially the part about children. But as time passed and no children appeared, the idea of being a homemaker lost much of its appeal for Babe.

George was wealthy. There was no need for Babe to continue working exhibitions. What she enjoyed was competing. But there was almost no competition in the women's professional golf circuit.

All right. Then she would see to it that her amateur standing was returned. Was it possible?

George thought it was. In January of 1940, Babe applied for reinstatement.

The USGA agreed to restore her amateur ranking — if she would go through a three-year waiting period during which she accepted no money for appearances, exhibitions, or anything else connected with golf. Was she willing to comply?

Was she? You bet! She would wait. In the meantime, there was plenty to do. George had just bought a bowling alley.

She would try bowling.

Then came December 7, 1941. Japanese bombers attacked an American naval base at Pearl Harbor in Hawaii, killing nearly 2,500 American soldiers, sailors, and civilians.

On December 8, President Franklin Roosevelt asked for immediate action, and war was declared by Congress that same day. All able men between the ages of 18 and 45 were called into military service.

George was 33. He tried to enlist. But he weighed over 250 pounds now, and had what he and Babe called "very coarse" veins. He was turned down.

If he had been accepted, Babe intended to join the Women's Army Corps. As it was, she donated her time and talent to armed services charities and war bond rallies. Though her amateur standing as a golfer was restored in 1943, there were few sports events to enter. The world was too concerned with the defeat of Hitler to care much who won or lost a tournament. Then, too, many athletes were in the armed services.

Fortunately, Babe's brothers lived through the war years. Poppa did not. He died of a heart attack in 1943.

It was the first death in the Didrikson family, and it hit Babe hard. Other people died. She knew that. But not anyone she loved. True, Poppa was old and hadn't been well for a long time. Still . . . .

Babe, Lillie, Louis, Bubba, Dora, Nancy, Ole — none of the Didrikson children could keep back their tears. Only Momma remained dry-eyed. No one could understand it. After all she and Poppa had meant to each other, how could she be so calm?

If she cried and carried on, everyone would be worrying over her and she didn't want that, Momma explained. People were born to die from the first breath. Nobody had unlimited time on earth. But there was no need to fuss about it. God knew what was going on.

Momma's children looked at her in silence. Hannah Marie Olson Didrikson had iron in her spine. Uprooting, accident, illness, war, poverty, death — none was more than she could bear. Would any of them ever be as strong as she?

Momma herself died two years later, in 1945. After burying her, Babe and George moved to Denver. And on August 6 of that year, the first atomic bomb was dropped on Hiroshima, killing 74,000 people. A second, on August 9, almost wiped out the industrial city of Nagasaki, killing 260,000.

Like almost everyone else, Babe had mixed feelings. The deaths of thousands of people was shocking, horrible. But they were faceless and far away. Truly, Momma and Poppa's deaths had been more devastating. But in any case, the war was over. Now everyone could get back to living a normal life.

For Babe, a normal life meant starting on the tournament circuit again. That fall, she won her second Texas Women's Open title and was chosen "Woman Athlete of the Year" for the second time. (The first time she had received the award was in 1932 after the Olympics. She would be chosen again in 1946, 1947, and 1950.)

A string of tournaments began in the summer of 1946, ending with the National Women's Amateur in September. Babe's goal was to win it. And she did — by the second biggest margin in the history of the tournament.

When the season ended in October, Babe was ready to take a vacation and enjoy her new home in Denver. It was the first house she and George had owned. But George didn't think it wise. He urged her to go to Florida and continue the winning streak she had going.

Florida? She would go, Babe told him, but only if he came with her. She had never enjoyed being alone, and still didn't. Well, George said, he'd be with her when he could, all right? All right. Babe left for Florida.

After her 15th victory, Babe was again ready to quit for a while. And once again George persuaded her to continue. He said she should go to Scotland now, and play in the British Women's Amateur. She needed something like that to top off her wins in the U.S.

Scotland? So far? Babe shook her head. She wouldn't go alone, and she knew George could not take that much time off from his several businesses.

But no American woman had ever taken the British Women's Amateur, George told her.

Who could resist such a challenge? Not Babe. She went to Scotland to show the world what she could do.

She did well — very well indeed. The final match was between Babe and a woman named Jacqueline Gordon, a surprise British winner who had been beating everyone all week.

Jacqueline's drives weren't as long as Babe's. But she was more consistent, particularly in the close shots. She was two up at the noon break.

Then Babe settled down, concentrated, and took over. She could do whatever she wanted with the ball that afternoon. It sailed, slid, jumped, crept, dropped, smooth as a butternut, light as a fly.

When the match ended, the crowd stood for 15 minutes and applauded. An American had finally won the British Women's Amateur. What's more, she had done it with one hand tied behind her, figuratively speaking. Babe had chipped a bone in her left thumb several days before the tournament while practicing. Not wanting anyone to think she was trying to build up an advance alibi, she taped up her thumb, wore a glove over the bandage, took a pain killer, and said nothing.

This bit of news created a tremendous response from the Britishers, known for their own endurance under hard conditions.

Babe deeply appreciated their applause. To show her gratitude, she sang a little Scottish song, danced the Highland Fling, and, in a moment of sheer exuberance, hurdled over the wall that circled the clubhouse.

"Ah, lass, we won't be forgettin' you for a while," one admirer told her. When Babe's train pulled out of Edinburgh the next day, the platform was crowded with hundreds of people singing "Auld Lang Syne."

6

Countless bids for appearances followed Babe's triumphant return home. She refused them all, intending to remain an amateur. And she did for a while. But the offers kept getting more and more tempting.

Babe didn't really need more money. George could well afford the $15,000 a year in expenses to keep Babe on the amateur golf circuit. But both George and Babe knew what it was like to be poor. Both had been working since they were very young. Both had slaved at menial jobs. Money, especially easy money, was hard to refuse.

That's why, when a Hollywood executive offered Babe a movie deal, she accepted. All she had to do was make a series of ten golf shorts illustrating her technique. It would take a week or two at most. And for this she would be paid $300,000, more than most people made in a lifetime. How could she *not* accept?

George called a press conference and announced Babe's decision to turn pro once again.

Never one to do anything halfway, Babe accepted as many offers as possible. One month, she spent 17 exhausting nights on a plane, playing golf in one place, then flying on to the next. Besides the endless travel back and forth across the country, there were the hot summer nights in hotel rooms. Most had no air-conditioning. Babe often found it too uncomfortable to sleep.

The strain began to show. One evening, while flying home from an awards affair, she suddenly had a sharp pain in her left side. She'd had stomachaches before—from nerves, excitement, indigestion. This was different. Sharper. And there was swelling where the pain was. A strained muscle; nothing to worry about, Babe told herself.

She was more concerned about the lack of competition for woman golfers. Awards were fine. But what good was an athlete if there were no athletic events in which to compete? If you didn't compete, you dried up like a peach pit. Men had a pro circuit. Why couldn't there be a pro circuit for women?

George had been thinking the same thing, and began working on the problem late in 1948. In January of 1949, the Ladies' Professional Golf Association was formed.

Babe continued her nationwide exhibitions, trying to encourage women golfers to join the association. One of the golfers she met was a young woman named Betty Dodd. Betty soon became like a daughter to Babe.

Betty was from Texas, like Babe. And she was a fine golfer. She also played a pretty good guitar. Babe now played the harmonica at least as well as her old radio idol, Castor Oil Clarence. She and Betty often played duets for themselves—and for anyone else who would listen.

About this time, Babe and George moved to the Sky Crest Country Club outside of Chicago, where Babe became a teaching pro at a guaranteed annual salary of $20,000. She was pleased. It wasn't only the money. It was a victory for women golfers everywhere. No woman had ever filled such a position before.

Babe was determined to prove how well a woman could

40

teach, and put in long hours giving lessons. She was still appearing in exhibitions, too. And she was playing in more tournaments than ever, now that the pro circuit was catching on.

In 1951, George and Babe bought their own golf course in Tampa, Florida. This meant more work for Babe.

She enjoyed what she was doing. But physical activity wasn't as easy for her as it once had been. The pain and swelling in her left side was still bothering her.

George was worried, and kept urging her to see a doctor. He became truly alarmed at the 1953 Women's Open in Richmond, California. There he saw Babe wince, saw how her strength faded as the rounds continued, saw her end up in fifth place — too wracked with pain to care very much.

"Honey, you must take time out and find out what's wrong," he told her. Babe finally agreed.

Ever loyal to old friends, she went to see Dr. W. E. Tatum, the doctor in Beaumont, Texas, who had treated the Didrikson family for years.

A femoral hernia in the strangulated stage, Dr. Tatum said. An operation was necessary. One more week and it would kill her.

The hernia operation was a success. Babe began feeling better right away. A little tired, but that was to be expected. The tournament circuit closed down in November and December. She would take it easy, sleep late, lie in the sun, and by January have her old pep back and be ready to go again.

But no matter how much sleep she got, Babe was tired all the time. Her back ached. Food didn't taste right.

Well, she wasn't a kid anymore. People didn't snap back as fast at 38 as they did at 18. After all those years as a competitor, every muscle at one time or another had suffered from pulling, straining, ripping. The body was bound to become sore. That's what she kept telling herself. But underneath was a little nagging doubt, a hint of suspicion. One day she let it slip.

Coming off the course, feeling really tired, she said to her young friend Betty Dodd, "You know, Betty, I think I might have cancer."

A specialist in Fort Worth, whom Dr. Tatum recommended, confirmed her suspicion.

The doctor was kind, patient. Mrs. Zaharias had cancer of the rectum, he explained. It could be treated by an operation. All of the rectum would be removed. A new outlet for the bowel movement would be made on the left side of the abdomen. The procedure was called a colostomy.

The doctor brought out diagrams and pictures, pointed at first one, then another. He assured Babe and George that there was every reason to be hopeful, that a person with a colostomy could live a very normal life. Furthermore, with each passing day, more was being learned about cancer. More people were being cured. On and on he talked.

It was all a blur to Babe. She was so stunned, in fact, that the seriousness of her condition didn't hit her until she and George were out of the doctor's office and in the elevator.

"No . . . ." The word came out of her mouth, muffled, choked. She had *cancer.* She was going to die! Why? What had she done? Hadn't she always been good to her parents, loyal to her friends, generous, honest? Why had this happened to *her?*

George tried to comfort her, but he broke down. And it was Babe who told their relatives and friends the bad news.

"This is it. I have cancer. I have to have a 'costomy' or something," she told Betty Dodd.

Betty was calm. She knew what a colostomy was. She knew a woman who had had one.

Babe perked up. So, you could live through it, then?

Of course you could live through it, Betty told her. She offered to come to the hospital and keep Babe company — days, nights, whenever Babe wanted her.

The two were close. And both were able to face facts without going to pieces. George was not. He loved his wife very much, and refused even to think about the seriousness of her illness, much less talk with her about it. As concerned as she was, Betty could talk with Babe.

Everyone in the country was concerned. Messages poured in from coast to coast.

"I'm just leaving everything in the hands of God," Babe told her many well-wishers.

God had become important to Babe in the last few weeks. Though she had not been to church regularly in many years, she was certain there was a God. Heck, she didn't even understand how a radio worked. How could she figure out God? She couldn't. He was there. He knew what was going on. That's what counted. So why worry?

Before going up to surgery, Babe told George to put her golf clubs where she could see them. She would be using

them again soon, she announced firmly.

And she did. On July 31, three and a half months after her operation, Babe entered a tournament at the Tam O'Shanter Country Club in Niles, Illinois.

Could she make any kind of a showing? Her devoted fans were eager to find out.

Her opening drive sailed 250 yards straight down the fairway. The gallery screamed hysterically. The Babe was back! She could still outdrive any woman alive, and most men.

But her short game was off, way off. And at the sixth tee

she turned away, weak, trembling, with tears in her eyes.

"Come on, honey," George said. "You've had enough for today. Pick up your ball and we'll go back to the clubhouse."

"No." Babe stuck out her chin. "I don't pick up the ball. I never have and I never will."

She finished 15th that day.

Two days later, she played a second tournament, this time winding up in third place.

Even though she missed many tournaments, Babe still placed number six on the list of money-winners in the 1953 pro women's circuit. Most golfers would have been pleased. Babe was not. She had to be first. There was no settling for anything else.

In 1954 she was back to try again, placing seventh in the first tournament, second in the next. Then came the Serbin

Women's Open in Miami Beach.

Babe was running neck and neck with the famous Patty Berg. They were coming to the last hole. It was a long one with a par five.

Babe drove hard — into a grove of palm trees, beyond which was a trap. Could she get out of it?

The gallery was quiet. They weren't sure. Neither was Babe. Her back ached. Her legs felt like lead. The incision in her abdomen hurt. Drops of sweat beaded her forehead as she picked up a 4-iron.

Where did she want the ball to go? That was the question. All else was forgotten — the weakness, pain, ache, heaviness, everything. Then she swung.

The shot came off exactly right, landing on the fairway. A three-quarter shot with her 9-iron put the ball on the green. And two steady putts rolled it into the cup. Babe had done it.

It was her first win since the cancer operation.

Other championships followed, including the National Women's Open, which she won by a margin of 12 strokes. It was one of the greatest comebacks in the history of sport.

Babe Didrikson Zaharias had overcome odds that most people would have found insurmountable. Guts. That's what she had. People looked at her and wanted to cheer — or kneel. She was now a legend. The world was at her feet.

But then her back began aching again. An operation for a ruptured disc was performed on June 22, 1955. All was well until the end of July, when she began having new pains in her back.

Tests were ordered.

"Cancer?" Babe said the word calmly. She had done a lot of thinking about cancer during the last year or so. It was still not a pretty word nor a pretty disease, but it was no worse than many others.

Yes, the doctors said, it was cancer. There was a trace of it on the right side of her sacrum, near the pelvis. They were going to try X-ray this time.

Should he put her clubs where she could see them, like the last time? George asked anxiously.

Yes, Babe said, bring the clubs. She had "whupped" cancer once. She could do it again, God willing.

And if God wasn't willing, what then?

George didn't, couldn't, ask the question. Babe asked it of herself. And she knew the answer. It was one she had learned from Momma years ago. You accepted God's decisions without making a fuss. Death was a part of life. There was nothing to be afraid of once you faced it.

In the meantime, she wasn't going to take any soupy sympathy.

Babe hung on for a while, smiling, even joking when visitors came. But a few months later she lapsed into a coma and died in her sleep.

There may have been equally talented athletes. And there may have been those equally colorful, dedicated, and courageous. But one who had all these qualities and could also play the harmonica as well as Castor Oil Clarence? Not likely.

Time Line for Babe Didrikson Zaharias

1913 — Babe Didrikson is born in Port Arthur, Texas, on June 26.

1930 — Babe Didrikson breaks three world records in the national Amateur Athletic Union championships.

1932 — Babe Didrikson wins two gold medals in the Olympic Games.

1932 — Babe Didrikson is chosen "Woman Athlete of the Year."

1932 — The AAU declares Babe Didrikson a professional.

1934 — Babe Didrikson wins the Texas State Women's Championship in golf.

1938 — Babe Didrikson marries George Zaharias on December 23.

1945 — Babe Didrikson Zaharias is chosen "Woman Athlete of the Year."

1946 — Babe Didrikson Zaharias is chosen "Woman Athlete of the Year."

1946 — Babe Didrikson Zaharias wins the National Women's Amateur.

1946 — Babe Didrikson Zaharias becomes the first American to win the British Women's Amateur.

1947 — Babe Didrikson Zaharias is chosen "Woman Athlete of the Year."

1950 — Babe Didrikson Zaharias is chosen "Woman Athlete of the Year."

1954 — Babe Didrikson Zaharias undergoes cancer surgery.

1954 — Babe Didrikson Zaharias wins the Serbin Women's Open.

1954 — Babe Didrikson Zaharias wins the National Women's Open.

1956 — Babe Didrikson Zaharias dies of cancer.